The

PARENT'S
GUIDE

Also by Dr. Keith Bell

Books
>The Swim To Win Playbook
>The Nuts & Bolts of Psychology for Swimmers
>Winning Isn't Normal
>Target on Gold
>Coaching Excellence
>You Only Feel Wet When You're Out of the Water
>Championship Sports Psychology
>What It Takes: The ABC's of Excelling

Audio Tape & CD
>Relaxation Training

The

PARENT'S GUIDE

to the

Proper Psychological Care and Feeding

of

the Competitive Swimmer

Dr. Keith Bell

Library of Congress Cataloging-in-Publication Data

3 1257 01367 6977

Bell, Keith F.
  The parent's guide to the proper psychological care and
  feeding of the competitive swimmer / Keith Bell
    p. cm.
  ISBN 0-945609-48-5
  1. Swimmers—Psychology. 2. Swimming for children
  —Psychological aspects. 3. Parent and child. I. Title
GV837.2.B43 2000
797.2'1'019—dc21 00-067171

Cover by Sandy Neilson-Bell, Keith Bell, and Bridger Bell

Printed in the United States of America

10 9 8 7 6 5 4 3 2 1

This book is available at a special discount when ordered in bulk quantities.

Published and distributed by:

Keel Publications

P.O. Box 160155
Austin, Texas 78716 U.S.A.
512-327-1280
www.swimdoc.com

for
Kirsten, Keena, Bridger, Cooper, Kaila,
and young, aspiring swimming champions everywhere

Competitive Swimming: The Preferred Choice

I used to kid myself. I used to pretend I didn't care what my children were doing as long as they were actively engaged in some activity that promoted personal growth.

I had hoped they would swim. Swimming is such a big part of my life. And I love it. But I told myself that it didn't really matter what they did as long as they were doing something: playing some sport, playing a musical instrument, engaging in a hobby, working a job, or otherwise busy with some productive activity.

I didn't want them idling away their time, getting bored, watching television, playing video games, or endlessly surfing the net (though they certainly could spend some good time on the computer surfing the world wide web to find a cure for cancer, pursuing venture capital for a start-up Internet company, or the like).

I figured doing something useful would aid their development. At the very least, if they kept meaningfully occupied, they would be more likely to stay out of trouble.

I did want some of their time to be devoted to getting some exercise. I wanted them to stay healthy and to value taking care of their bodies. Beyond that, I didn't care what they were doing as long as they were doing something healthy and were striving to do whatever it was they were doing extremely well. Or so I told myself.

Since my wife and I are totally immersed in the swimming world (both of us coach swimming and swim competitively, and I play sports psychologist for swimming teams all over the world), it was easy to direct my children into this sport that we love. Swimming was the natural thing to do in our family.

Oh, they did some other things. At one time or another, one or another of them (or all of them) has played volleyball, baseball, soccer, karate, tennis, golf, guitar, and/or piano. My daughters, Kirsten and Keena, worked paying jobs all through high school and college. Bridger, my older son, composes classical music. And they all surf the net. Fortunately, they all also chose to swim. They love it.

I say "fortunately" because I was deluding myself. I did care. I wanted them to swim. I still do.

Swimming is incredible. There may not be any better way to spend time than totally engaged in the pursuit of competitive swimming excellence. The rewards are that rich.

CONTENTS

PART I
THE BENEFITS

Chapter 1

Competitive Swimming: The Best Choice

Competitive swimming: an opportunity of riches

Competitive swimming presents an amazing array of rich rewards to its participants. It offers a completely engaging, fun, exciting, growth-producing, healthy lifestyle set in a wonderfully wholesome environment. Moreover, it offers some very unique and special opportunities that cannot be found anywhere else.

Swimming does the body good. Swimming offers its participants unparalleled opportunity to achieve phenomenal fitness and tremendous physical strength. In fact, regular training for competitive swimming guarantees a lifetime of fitness with extremely minimal risk of injury.

Swimming gives its participants a head start on the rest of life. Swimming offers unparalleled opportunity for maximal personal growth and development. The competitive swimming experience uniquely lends itself to the acquisition and development of a wide variety of life skills; skills that readily transfer to all aspects of life, including educational and vocational pursuits.

Competitive swimming is a good, clean, wholesome pastime. Typically, competitive swimming fosters a number of healthy values.

Competitive swimming is a pool full of fun. As good as it is for its participants, swimming is still play. Swimmers reap incredible rewards merely by playing competitive swimming. Swimming is fun, exciting, challenging, and, often, downright thrilling.

Competitive swimming: the opportunity of a lifetime

Swimming offers a means for a lifetime of health and fitness. When your child gets in the swim, he not only learns the skills, values, and habits that can be applied to sustain success, health, and fitness throughout his life; but he is introduced to a sport in which he can continue to play as long as he lives. Swimming is not merely preparation for the rest of life, it is a wonderful part of life.

Anyone can play swimming all of his life. Competitive swimming is not only child's play. Adults can play too.

In how many other sports can one actively compete in the golden, or should I say silver-haired, years? Few persons play football, basketball, or baseball in their eighties or nineties; whereas many swim for health, fitness, and enjoyment (and some actively train and compete in swimming) throughout their entire lives. Swimming offers competitive opportunities in age groups from 6-and-under to 100-and-over.

Meanwhile, while playing, swimmers forge close friendships that last forever. Competitive swimming truly is the opportunity of a lifetime.

Competitive swimming: it does the body good

Swimmers train harder than any other athletes in the world. That is not to say that athletes in other sports do not devote as much time and attention to their sports as swimmers do. They do. It's just that swimmers train with greater physical intensity.

Swimmers train as hard as they do because they can. They can, because there is virtually no risk of injury in swimming. If other athletes were to train as hard as swimmers do, they would get hurt.

Swimmers train in this soft, cool medium called "water." They train lying down, cushioned, cooled, refreshed, buoyed, and caressed by the water. In order to swim, swimmers must merely strive to grab this elusive liquid and propel their bodies forward through this forgiving substance as it gracefully yields to their momentum and moves aside to let them through. With each stroke, they gently slide their hands into the water (meeting resistance only from the surface tension, drag from the bottom of the pool, and the gentle weight of the flowing water), barely nudging the water as it moves out of the way to allow the hand to enter. Most other sports require repeated, semi-violent collisions with solid, ungiving, and unforgiving surfaces.

While other athletes frequently face the damaging effects of heat—overheating with effort, dehydration, heat exhaustion, and sometimes even flirting with heat stroke—the cool water serves as a buffer against these dangers. Even in the hottest of swimming pools, the water is significantly cooler than the body's natural state. The water constantly cools swimmers' bodies, effectively removing the danger of radical overheating and its resultant heat exhaustion and heat stroke.

Moreover, swimming is done lying down. Swimmers do not have to fight gravity or deal with the risk of falling and crashing to the ground. The risk of injury from swimming is almost non-existent.

Because it is possible to train incredibly hard without fear of injury, some swimmers do. In so doing, they throw down the gauntlet and raise the bar, inviting others to train hard in order to compete. Many accept the challenge, making it necessary for others also to prepare well in order to compete.

As a result of repeatedly meeting these rare physical challenges, enormous adaptation takes place. Phenomenal cardiopulmonary systems are produced. Muscle strength is vastly increased. Swimmers' bodies become beautiful, inordinately powerful, efficient, enduring machines.

Even the mild (by comparison) challenges, introduced to more novice swimmers, engender extraordinary levels of fitness and physical development. More swimming and faster swimming (especially during the the growing years) pays even greater dividends.

Swimming is the best exercise one can get. It is the ultimate fitness activity. Competitive swimming engenders fitness, power, stamina, flexibility, and robust health. Swimming produces the best-looking, healthiest bodies in the world. Competitive swimming truly does the body good.

Competitive swimming: the ultimate fix

Swimming may not be a panacea, but it is the exercise of choice for:
- asthma
- arthritis
- strengthening the heart and lungs
- rehabilitating injuries.

Swimming is relaxing, destressing, rejuvenating, and healing.

Competitive swimming: good, clean fun

Swimmers play a clearly-defined, easily-understood, somewhat simple, game where there is little exploitation and practically no cheating. Swimming is a game where most of the rewards come from the quest, not the conquest, from playing to win, not from having won. As a result, there is no need to step on anyone else in order to get to the top. It is all good, clean, fun.

Competitive swimming: it builds good, wholesome values

Competitive swimming teaches good, wholesome values. Among other ideals, swimmers learn to value:
- personal responsibility
- the pursuit of excellence
- superlative preparation
- commitment
- fair play
- respect for others
- healthy competition
- the worthy opponent
- opportunity
- lifetime fitness
- resources
- long-term planning and investment
- health

Competitive swimming: a child's safe haven

Competitive swimming provides a great way to keep tabs on your child. If your child is a swimmer, it is most likely that you know where he is most of the time. Because excellence demands a lot of time, most competitive swimming teams offer many hours of instruction, practice, and competition to their participants. Swimmers, depending on their ages, current achievement levels, and commitment, typically spend between three and thirty hours per week swimming. That does not include the time spent at meets, travel to and from practice, and adjunct activities. Competitive swimming is a lifestyle—a tremendously fun, exciting, and healthy one at that.

While your child is swimming, he is engaged in the common pursuit of noble, lofty goals with others with similar values under the watchful eyes of caring professionals. What is more, competitive swimming is virtually injury free and devoid of cheating.

When he is swimming, your child is busy getting fit; acquiring, developing, and honing a wide variety of life skills; having a pool full of fun, and—you know where he is, and what he is doing, most all of the time.

Competitive swimming: the feel-good sport

Swimming just plain feels good: the cool, smooth sensation of the water against one's skin, the gentle cushion against gravity that the water supplies as it supports the swimmer's body, the flow of the water rushing past the swimmer as he powers through it, the exhilarating feel of exertion and its resulting speed. It feels good to immerse the body in the water. It feels good to propel the body through the water.

The game is fun to play. It's fun to race. It's fun to tackle the challenges. It's fun to compete against others, against the clock, and against oneself.

It's fun to train. Every drill can be a game. Everyone gets to play all of the time.

Swimming unfailingly offers opportunity to play. There are always new games to play, new competition to conquer, faster speeds to challenge, and new techniques to master. And, there are many other nice swimmers with whom to play.

It is fun and exciting to challenge one's body, to exercise decision-making skills, to explore pace and strategy, and to strive to swim faster than one's previous best and faster than anyone else.

Swimming is a game where no one ever loses. Not everyone wins, but everyone benefits.

Swimming presents a pool full of fun. It is the feel-good sport.

Competitive swimming: it's for everyone

In swimming, anyone can play. Swimming is blind to race, creed, color, socioeconomic status, gender, age, ability, and disability. Swimming is for:

- boys and girls
- men and women
- young and old
- rich and poor
- beginner and expert
- the healthy, the infirm, and the disabled

Not only can anyone play swimming, but everyone who swims gets to play almost all of the time. In most swimming meets everyone plays. No one sits out and warms the bench. During swimming practices everyone is involved and active almost the entire time. There is very little standing around watching or waiting one's turn. Swimmers play the entire time.

Competitive swimming: it guarantees success

Swimming is easy. Children readily learn to swim. With a little instruction and a modicum of training, swimmers quickly gain vast proficiency in this physical art. In fact, in practically no time at all, your tyro competitive swimmer will swim better and faster than 99.99% of the world's population.

Competitive swimming: it provides unlimited challenge

Swimming is difficult. Swimming is competed at an extraordinarily high level of excellence. Its challenges are enormous. To compete at the higher levels of the sport, one must acquire and maintain extraordinary levels of fitness. One must become highly-skilled and must exhibit considerable expertise at preparation and execution-upon-demand under a wide variety of conditions.

Swimming provides constant, multi-level challenges to fit every child's situation. There are always new goals to set and new games to play. Even if your swimmer makes it to the top of the sport, there are always faster speeds to challenge and new techniques to master. There is always new, up-and-coming, blossoming competition to conquer.

Competitive swimming: it's not just a game, it's an adventure

Swimming is like Star Trek. The whole idea is for your swimmer to:

- explore new worlds
- experience swimming speeds never before found
- take his body to places few, or no, others ever go
- regularly do things he has never done before
- search the galaxy for ways to boldly go where no man has ever gone before.

Competitive swimming: an incredible bargain

The cost of taking advantage of what your local swimming team offers will vary from place to place, from time to time, and will depend upon your child's level of participation. Generally, however, compared to other sports, to other activities, and even to child care; swimming teams are amazing bargains—especially when you consider the nature of the sport, the benefits derived, and how much time, expert instruction, and close supervision your child is afforded. You cannot do better. Competitive swimming is a great deal.

Competitive swimming: a cut above the rest

Your local Swimming Club provides:
- professional coaches
- expert instruction at all levels
- constant supervision
- peer support
- parental involvement

Chapter 2

The Lessons

Competitive swimming: a head start on the rest of life

Swimming provides the impetus for the acquisition, development, and refinement of skills that are readily applied for success in a wide variety of life's pursuits. In fact, because of the combination of the quest for superlative performance, the clarity and exactness of measurement of performance, and the immediacy and omnipresence of performance feedback; swimming lends itself to the acquisition, development, and refinement of life skills better than any other endeavor.

Moreover, there are no consequences for failure built into the game of swimming. There is nothing to lose. The vast majority of the wealth of benefits that come from playing swimming accrue from playing, not from having won. As a result, swimmers are free to give it a go, to creatively explore a wide variety of strategies, thereby building a powerful arsenal of skills.

Of course, the more consistently your child pursues swimming excellence, the more he benefits. It is playing to win, not just playing, that triggers the greatest payoff.

Swimming naturally lends itself to the development of life skills. So too do good personal skills promote swimming excellence. As a result, many swimming coaches devote special attention to providing swimmers with opportunity directed at such skill acquisition. They infuse their training programs with life skills building activities and often arrange for additional resources (books, clinics, etc.) to supplement such training.

The lessons provided are rich. Swimmers learn:
- to dream
- to set goals skillfully
- to take advantage of opportunity
- to act now
- to pursue excellence passionately
- to get to know themselves
- to make good decisions
- to manage time
- to utilize positive self-talk
- to exhibit a positive attitude
- to cooperate with others in pursuit of common goals
- to treat everyone with respect and dignity

- to plan, prepare, and rehearse
- to delay gratification
- to utilize resources
- to resist peer pressure
- to perform under pressure
- to handle failure
- to understand that life is not fair
- to judge performance, not Self
- to take appropriate risks
- to make the pursuit of excellence fun

To dream

Swimmers learn to imagine the unimaginable; to dream new paths, new means, new worlds; to see beyond obstacles, how to get through them, over them, around them, to make the obstacles cease to exist; and to see what could be, what may be, and what will be. Swimmers learn to dream the dreams that inspire, power, and maintain the pursuit of excellence. They learn to create sparks within, to pursue their dreams, and to find ways to make their dreams into realities.

To set goals skillfully

Competitive swimming provides the clearest of goals: victory. The object of the sport is pure and simple: to swim a particular stroke a specified distance faster than anyone else. Electronic measurement leaves no doubt as to the results.

Everything a swimmer does either is measured or can be measured. Races are timed—to the one hundredth of a second. Practice swims are timed (or, at least, there is almost always a pace clock running from which a swimmer may assess his performance.) Heart rate can be monitored. Distance covered can be tracked. Strokes can be counted. And stroke rate can be calculated.

Performances can be compared against a swimmer's previous swims, those of teammates, others' times in meets, and times recorded in competitions across the state, the country, and internationally. Times can be compared to historical performances, measured against existing records, and compared to qualifying standards for future meets.

There is little, if anything, else in life in which performance is so clearly measured and immediate feedback so regularly available. A swimmer is constantly provided with information as to what he did, how well he did it, and how his performance compares to others in a wide variety of classifications.

Armed with this information and with the aid of their coaches' expertise, swimmers come upon some ever-changing ideas of what levels of performance are good (for them in their present circumstances and compared to others.) This makes competitive swimming the perfect arena for the acquisition, development, refinement, and utilization of goal setting skills.

To take advantage of opportunity

Opportunity is always limited. It is there and then it is gone, never to present itself again. Those that jump on opportunity leap forward ahead of the competition.

In swimming, the relationship between making the most of opportunity and success is plain to see for anyone who cares to notice. Swimmers learn to take advantage of opportunity.

To act now

Swimming provides constant deadlines. It makes it difficult to put things off for later.

Your swimmer will not be able to put off his training for when he feels like it. Practice will go on whether or not he attends.

When the starter beeps the horn to start the race, there is no deciding when to go. The time to act is now. The lesson is clear: the competition does not wait around.

To pursue excellence passionately

There is so much to love about swimming. It is fun. It feels good. It is exhilarating and vivifying.

Swimmers quickly tend to learn to embrace high aspirations and to get passionate about this exciting, enjoyable quest. It is easy to do when they become part of a special group that is immersed in the daily pursuit of excellence. For one thing, your swimmer will encounter others who have decided to pursue their goals with great fervor and intensity. The passion is contagious. Your swimmer can catch it and release it in any arena.

To get to know themselves

Swimmers have great opportunity for self-discovery. The water provides a protective cocoon, built for only one, surrounding each swimmer, leaving him alone with himself and his thoughts.

The game of competitive swimming comes complete with formidable challenges and requires frequent tough decisions. It is a very personal thing. How well one does, how high one aspires, how one handles the challenges, and the decisions one makes are all intimate issues. A swimmer gets much opportunity to learn a tremendous amount about how he handles himself.

To make good decisions

Swimming promotes good decision-making skills. Swimmers learn to make choices based upon long-term benefit. They learn about commitment; and the advantages of making decisions in advance rather than on the whim of the moment, competing alternatives, immediate distractions, or others' values.

To manage time

Competitive swimming is tightly contested at an extraordinarily high level of excellence. In order to compete successfully, swimmers play hard and long, devoting many hours to their sport.

With so much of the day regularly devoted to school and swimming, swimmers quickly become proficient at managing their time. They have little choice. They learn to prioritize, to schedule, and to act efficiently and productively.

To utilize positive self-talk

While your child is swimming, there is no one for him to talk to but himself. What he chooses to say to himself profoundly affects the quality of his experience and his level of performance. Swimming demonstrates the effectiveness of self-instructional methods, mood-enhancing self-statements, positive expectancies, and a positive attitude.

To exhibit a positive attitude

Swimming performance is determined by a combination of preparation and execution. Execution, both during preparation and at race time, is effected by attitude. Competitive swimming rewards the display of a positive attitude.

To cooperate with others in pursuit of common goals

Swimming practices require cooperative efforts. Swimmers must act together to accomplish sets in shared lanes. They help each other with getting times, counting laps and repeats, and with understanding complex instructions. They model stroke technique, pace off of each other, and race each other. They set standards, challenge each other, and raise the bar. The more they cooperate, the easier it is to get where they want to go.

To treat everyone with respect and dignity

Although swimmers tend to forge close friendships with the teammates with whom they share common goals, dreams, and experiences; they do not have to like each other. Swimming does, however, teach them that they have to treat each other with respect and dignity. If they do not, it is harder to succeed. Excellence flourishes in an atmosphere of respect.

To plan, prepare, and rehearse

Generally, it is not the best swimmer who wins. It is usually the swimmer who prepares and executes the best who wins. Swimming teaches the value of superlative preparation.

Swimmers quickly learn, for example, that they feel better in the water, have more fun, and swim faster for longer periods of time when they are in shape. It does not take long for swimmers to make the connection between training and its benefits. Swimming shows no favorites; rather it rewards superlative preparation.

To delay gratification

In this high-tech age there is so much opportunity for instant gratification that our youth have relatively little opportunity to learn to invest in long-term payoffs. Although swimming is instantly rewarding, being fun to play, many of the payoffs require long-term investments which provide no guarantees. Even in a sport where each day's practice is fun and rewarding to play, swimmers still learn the value of delaying gratification, while investing in a better future.

To utilize resources

No one can carry your swimmer to swimming excellence. The responsibility for his fate is his. He has to do it himself. Part of taking responsibility, however, is a strategic utilization of resources.

Swimmers are provided with coaches, teammates, and competitors from whom to learn. Coaches often expose swimmers to nutritionists, exercise physiologists, weight trainers, physicians, chiropractors, and, if the coaches are smart, sports psychologists with particular expertise in the application of their respective fields to swimming.

Swimmers are provided with a wide variety of swimming aids: pace clocks, kick boards, pull buoys, fins, and paddles, for example. Weight training apparatus, books, magazines, audio tapes, video tapes, and Internet resources are there to be utilized. The wise swimmer learns to utilize resources.

To resist peer pressure

Swimmers learn to dare to act differently. They have to. If they accede to peer pressure, they act like everyone else: normal, average, mediocre. In order to excel, they must resist peer pressure, take unusual action, and stand out from the crowd.

To perform under pressure

Although a select few swimmers may prosper financially from their swimming, swimming usually provides only modest material rewards even for those who excel. On the other hand, swimming provides nothing to lose for those who fail, while yielding benefits to all who play. It is all for fun. The vast majority of swimming's payoff accrues from playing to win, independent of the outcome.

Nevertheless, sometimes the stakes seem high. Society teaches us to put pressure on ourselves even in this win-win situation called "competitive swimming." Parents, coaches, teammates, fans, the media, and, subsequently, swimmers themselves bring pressure to what is just a game. As a result, swimmers have great opportunity to learn to perform in pressure situations, to put things in perspective, and to enjoy playing to win without concern for failure.

To handle failure

Swimmers repeatedly experience failure on a regular basis, but they do so in the context of playing a game. As such they have the opportunity to learn and to truly understand that failure is merely a gap between expectations and experience, that failure is merely the difference between one's goals (in this case, goals that are somewhat arbitrary and merely set the stage for a healthy challenge) and one's performance.

In fact, in this game, there are no aversive consequences delivered contingent upon failure. Instead, even if swimmers fail, they still get to play, have fun, learn from their mistakes, and reap most of the benefits of the sport.

Swimming helps its athletes learn that although failure is never the goal and is not worthy of their attention, failure is not terrible and having failed does not make them failures.

To understand that life is not fair

Swimmers quickly learn that life is not fair. Although he usually does, the swimmer who prepares the best or puts the most into the race, does not always win. It may not be fair, but that is the way it is.

Fortunately, swimming teaches the universal truth that life is not fair in the context of a game where, no matter who wins, everyone who plays benefits. This makes accepting this often unpleasant reality a little easier.

To judge performance, not Self

Although it is one of the most formidable psychological challenges swimmers face (see pp. 69-71), swimmers have great opportunity to learn to judge their performances without putting their egos on the line. Swimming regularly provides the experience that demonstrates the need for learning to separate performance from self-worth, highlights the issues involved in understanding this problem, and provides continual opportunity to practice judging one's performance without rating one's Self.

To take appropriate risks

Competitive swimming provides an ideal arena for risk-taking behavior. In swimming, there are no consequences for failure. There is virtually no risk of injury. And, the vast majority of the rewards come from the relentless pursuit of victory independent of others' performances. Swimmers are free to explore many different strategies. There is nothing to lose.

To make the pursuit of excellence fun

Swimming is exciting. Swimming is fun. And, while swimming is a game, the pursuit of swimming excellence becomes quite serious play.

Swimmers devote many concerted hours to developing and refining superlative skills and building and maintaining incredibly fit, powerful bodies while striving to swim faster than anyone else; but they do so in the context of playing a game they enjoy and love. Swimmers learn to combine superlative action with enjoyment. They learn to make the pursuit of excellence fun.

Chapter 3

The Virtues

Competitive swimming: it builds character

Competitive swimming promotes the actions that support excellence in any endeavor. Swimming fosters:

- personal responsibility
- independence
- consistency
- persistence
- resolve
- leadership
- confidence
- self-reliance
- dedication, determination, desire, and discipline
- assertiveness
- integrity
- teamwork

Personal responsibility

As everyone knows, you can lead a horse to water, but you can't make him swim a 200 fly. Competitive swimming offers an unparalleled wealth of opportunity, but, as with anything, your swimmer must take responsibility for taking advantage of the opportunity and for reaping the rewards.

One of the magnificent opportunities swimming offers is the opportunity to realize responsibility. Every swimmer has the opportunity to learn to take responsibility for his own experience. Swimming teaches that it is up to each individual swimmer to see to it that he has fun, swims fast, competes effectively, and gets the most out of this very special opportunity.

Not everyone gets it. Some will choose to go hungry at an already-paid-for, all-you-can-eat buffet. But the opportunity to learn to take responsibility is there. And swimming is a great teacher.

Independence

Competitive swimming will provide your child with constant supervision, clear guidance, and an abundance of great resources. Professional coaches will plan and guide almost every step of the preparation and planning for competition. But when it comes time to race, no one can do it for the swimmer. He has to do it all himself.

In many ways, a coach's job is to put himself out of work, to prepare swimmers to do it themselves. Competitive swimming teaches the skills that foster independence.

Consistency

Contrary to what many think, it does not take extraordinary efforts to generate great performances. Performance excellence comes with doing things that are readily accomplished, but doing them consistently well. Excellence comes with taking care of the little things—the details that others neglect.

For the most part, the things it takes to win are not that hard to do. The hard part is consistently doing the little things well. Swimming rewards consistency.

Persistence

Swimming rewards persistence. To those who stay with it and keep after it, swimming practically assures at least a modicum of success. This lesson is easy to see and readily modeled. Moreover, swimming coaches tend to be great at providing opportunity to persist.

Resolve

Though fun, rich, and rewarding, the challenges swimming provides are difficult. The road to excellence is bumpy, filled with steep hills to climb, and sprinkled with potholes. Swimmers inevitably will experience temporary setbacks.

Swimmers learn to keep going, to let nothing stand in the way. There just is something about deep water that promotes the resolve to get to the other end.

Leadership

Swimmers are repeatedly given the opportunity to develop leadership skills. Whether breaking a record, leading his lane, demonstrating a stroke drill, leading a cheer, or being the first to make an interval or to post a time, a swimmer constantly leads. Swimming is very much about exploring the unknown, paving the way, being first—leading.

Confidence

Swimming builds confidence. Anyone who swims, quickly acquires the capacity to swim well. In very little time, with the ready acquisition of even the most rudimentary of skills and a modicum of conditioning; your child swims better than does the vast majority of the world's population.

Swimmers do this thing called "swimming," that most everyone they know does with at least some regularity, but they do it better than almost everyone else, readily experiencing immediate success. Their swimming competence engenders feelings of self-efficacy and confidence.

Moreover, contrary to popular belief, confidence is not something that one has or does not have. Confidence is something one does. Swimmers are taught to do confidence and they are taught how to do it.

Self-reliance

Especially as swimmers graduate to year-round swimming teams, they are exposed to professional coaches. These coaches are expert resource persons who provide great structure to training and to the game. They manage practice, set standards, teach skills, and control both the environment and much of the opportunity. But, as mentioned above, no one, not even the best of professional coaches, can do it for the swimmers. Swimming teaches young athletes to rely on themselves. Not only that, it teaches them that they can rely on themselves.

The competitive swimming environment allows swimmers to experience self-reliance. Swimming quickly provides them with fitness, skills, strength, and resolve to do phenomenal physical tasks. It teaches them personal skills with which to meet life's psychological challenges. Swimming demonstrates to its athletes their efficacy and their power, giving them good reason to rely upon themselves and the confidence with which to do so.

Dedication, determination, desire, and discipline

Swimming teaches its athletes the benefits of goal-oriented decisions, thereby promoting the exhibition of the consistent action that is often thought of as dedication, desire, determination, and discipline. Swimming teaches much about how to get things done, how to do things well, and how to outperform the competition.

Assertiveness

No one gets carried to excellence. So, swimmers are taught to take care of themselves, to go after what they want with respect and value for others.

Swimmers are taught the value of taking charge. They are taught to find a way to make it happen.

In a sport devoid of aggression, where the athletes are separated by lane lines and cannot interfere with, or otherwise effect, each other's opportunity, swimmers learn to assertively go after what they want.

Integrity

A swimmer cannot cheat and win. First of all, it is extremely difficult to cheat in swimming, where the task is clear, pure, and simple. A swimmer races practically naked, under the watchful eyes of many officials, teammates, coaches, and spectators.

Yes, extremely few have cheated by utilizing banned substances to enhance performance. Some have even gotten away with it, but they did not win. They may have appeared to have won if they did not get caught, but they did not win. They merely played a different game.

Most poignant, however, is the fact that swimming is so much about personal bests that not only must it be done well, but it must be done fairly and ethically in order for a swimmer to be pleased. There is no deceiving excellence. Its essence is only achieved with honesty and integrity.

Teamwork

Competitive swimming is said to be an individual sport, but in many ways it does more to promote teamwork than the so-called "team" sports. As mentioned above, swimming requires cooperative action. Moreover, teamwork comes from individual action. Teams get built when individuals consistently contribute to the team's mission. Competitive swimming provides an atmosphere of cooperation, clear goals, expectancy of contribution, and respect; all of which produces teamwork.

PART II
THE TEAM

Chapter 4

Selecting the Best
Swimming Team for Your Child

Get clear on your goals

Now that you know what competitive swimming has to offer and you have decided to provide your child with this great opportunity, get clear on your goals for your child. As Yogi Berra once said, "If you don't know where you are going, when you get there you'll be lost."

Why do you want your child to swim? What is your purpose in providing him with this opportunity?

What do you want your child to get out of swimming? What do you want him to accomplish?

Is competitive swimming something you use as a baby-sitting service, an alternative to after school care? Is it merely an activity, something to keep your child busy and out of trouble? Do you view swimming as an opportunity for your child to earn a scholarship to pay for his college education? Do you perceive competitive swimming to be an exercise program where your child can attain and maintain a modicum of, or superlative, fitness? Do you want your child to learn to compete successfully in the world: to acquire, develop, and hone life skills? Will your child share in the Olympic dream?

Get clear on what you want your child to get out of his swimming. Then provide him with the best opportunity to get it.

What should you look for in a swimming team?

In some areas, there is only one game in town. If you want your child to get to play, sign him up.

In other locales there are numerous swimming teams from which to choose. You merely need to decide which program is the best one for your child.

Convenience is always an issue. Practice times, geographic proximity, others with whom to carpool; these things are real. They count. At some point, however, you may wish to look more deeply into what each program has to offer.

You are investing in your child's life; in his present and in his future. As they say in the investing world, do your due diligence. Check out where a team has been, where it is going, and what it has to offer.

What is the team's mission statement, its philosophy? What supervision and protections are provided for your child? Has this program been recommended by others whose opinions you value? What has been the quality of others' experiences with this team? What are the team's achievements? What is its history?

Do swimmers from the team go on to swim in college and beyond? Do they continue to swim as adults, perhaps in Masters competition?

Are the swimmers enjoying themselves? Do they enjoy the training, the meets, and the interaction with staff and teammates?

Examine the coaches' credentials. Interview the head coach and the coach in whose group your child will swim. How much experience do the coaches have? What are their philosophies? What honors and achievements have they notched? Have any professional complaints been registered against them?

What costs are involved? What is expected of the parents? Are there volunteer commitments? What will be your financial commitment? What expectations are placed on the swimmers?

Talk to parents who previously have had children on the team as well as parents whose children are presently involved in the program. Ask them about their children's experience. Ask them what to ask.

Fortunately, swimming programs have so much to offer that, no matter which team you choose, it is hard to go wrong. And, of course, you can always help to make your child's team even better.

Swimming teams cannot be all things to everyone

Some teams are consumer-oriented. They strive to please everyone: to be all things to all comers.

When teams try to please everyone, they fail to do anything extremely well. They are too scattered. They stumble along with little sense of direction. They change with new boards of directors, different coaches, and evolving membership. They react to the winds of social change.

These teams are so busy trying to please everyone that they are confused about the nature of what they have to offer. They never get around to identifying their mission, or, if they do, they lose their identities and values chasing everyone's momentary approval. As a result, these teams tend to struggle much of the time.*

Other teams have some purpose, a mission, a reason to exist. They have clearly defined mission statements. They concentrate on what they have to offer. Subsequently, they thrive.

Look for a team that knows where it is going and what it has to offer.

---

* Please note, however, that no matter that many programs fail in one way or another, the vast majority of them still do many things well. Moreover, competitive swimming is so rich in what it has to offer that your child is likely to benefit tremendously from his experience, even in the worst of swimming programs.

The mission of choice: to provide opportunity for the pursuit of competitive swimming excellence

Like any good organization, a team should have a clearly identified mission. Of course, different teams may have different mandates, different missions, different reasons for existing.

Some missions work much better than others. Some are particularly suited to the sport of competitive swimming.

A swimming team, by its very nature, is at least partially dedicated to providing the opportunity for swimmers to pursue excellence in competitive swimming. The nature of the sport is "competitive" swimming.

While others might not agree, I think that "to provide opportunity for the pursuit of competitive swimming excellence" is the mission of choice for any swimming team. Moreover, I can confidently assert that the opportunity to pursue competitive excellence is the essence of the sport. Therefore, there will be at least some elements of this mission within every program.

Even if the mission statement proclaims something about "building character," "reaching potential," "being the best you can be," or the like; there still will be a consistent underlying movement toward the pursuit of competitive excellence (which, of course, will go a long way toward helping youngsters "build character," "reach potential," "be the best they can be," and contribute to the fulfillment of many other good intentions). Swimmers will be asked to, and helped to, swim faster. How much faster will be largely defined by the competitive environment.

Even in those programs that profess merely to be interested in participation (participation in what?) or personal progress and that eschew competition; the amount of personal progress that is deemed to be "good," the level of challenges set forth in training, the techniques and training methods utilized, and the standards set all will be substantially determined by the competitive environment. The competition will define what is good, even for the individual in relation to his own past performance.

Look for a team that acknowledges that the greatest benefits derive from the quest for swimming excellence; a team that knows that the particular opportunity a "competitive" swimming team offers is, by its very nature, the opportunity to pursue excellence in competitive swimming. Hopefully, your local team recognizes the inevitable and embraces a mission statement that emphasizes "providing the opportunity for the pursuit of excellence in competitive swimming."

In any case, it pays for every competitive swimmer to recognize, adopt, and value the pursuit of competitive swimming excellence. He will get much more out of his swimming experience if he does.

And while you, as a parent, may not hold the pursuit of competitive swimming excellence as the highest priority as yet, you will do well to recognize that the sport is "competitive" swimming and that the object of the game is to win. (You will, at some level, care about your child's comparative performance—if for no other reason than the fact that he will.) You will do well to value competition and the pursuit of excellence. You will do well to embrace this mission (or its hidden role in what the team has to offer). Keep this in mind when selecting a team for your child.

It is the pursuit, not the attainment

Competitive swimming is very much about the pursuit of excellence. To some this is scary. It is scary because we are acutely aware of how preciously few will excel. But the true value of competitive swimming is not steeped in excelling. Though excellent performance has its rewards, most of the value that accrues from competitive swimming is generated by the pursuit of excellence. The chase is more replete with reward than is even the conquest.

It is the pursuit of excellence that promotes fitness, health, good values, clean living, life skills, and many of the other beneficial by-products that accrue from playing competitive swimming right.

Not many excel, but everyone can pursue excellence. And everyone benefits greatly from being engaged in such a lofty pursuit.

Making the pursuit of swimming excellence fun

Competitive swimming is tremendous fun. It is fun to swim. It is fun to race. It is fun to take on difficult challenges and to engage every aspect of human capacity in the battle.

The challenges are tough. But there are great rewards to be had in tackling these challenges. The pursuit of excellence is a rich and rewarding pursuit. As such, it is unlikely that your team's mission is solely to have fun. There is a lot more value to competitive swimming than just the fun. However, the pursuit of competitive excellence should be made fun. It only makes sense.

A team should take care to make and keep the pursuit of swimming excellence fun. The pursuit of excellence should not be devoid of enjoyment. Neither should enjoyment be allowed to get in the way of the pursuit of excellence. Such a mission is too valuable.

There is a huge difference between making the pursuit of excellence fun and having fun at the expense of the pursuit of competitive excellence. The opportunity provided is for the pursuit of excellence. Care should be taken to make this pursuit fun without letting the fun get in the way of the mission.

What can you expect from the program?

I recently listened to a parent complain about a requirement put out by the coach. The parent was incensed, complaining that the coach "is my employee."—Well, no; that is not the case.

A coach may be the employee of an organization run by a board of directors. That, however, does not make him your employee, even if you are on the board. You do well to realize that you pay a team (and its coaches) for a service (defined by them, not by you) to be provided to your child. The team (and its coaching staff) is not obligated to continue to accept payment for that service any more than you are obligated to continue to pay for the service beyond any agreed-upon contract. There may be certain requirements, policies, boundaries, guidelines, and, most certainly, fees with which you and your child must comply in order to continue to qualify to receive the opportunity for your child to get to play. Most certainly, the team is not obligated (neither are its coaches) to mold the service to fit the needs of your child, or what you want for your child, let alone your momentary whims and desires .

You do well to select the program that best fits what you want for your child and that offers a service you like; recognizing that no team is perfect, no team will be perfectly suited for you or your child, and that everything changes. Moreover, the team, its directors (if it is that kind of organization), and its coaches seek to provide a particular, narrowly-defined service (most notably: the opportunity for the pursuit of excellence in competitive swimming) to a small portion of the population.

While coaches tend to care about each and every child on the team (including yours) and, want each child to have a good, healthy, growth-producing experience, to swim fast, and to win; they are responsible for the overall program and for all of its members. Sometimes this may mean that others' interests must come before yours. Certainly, it means that the integrity of the program and its mission must take precedence over anything that you may want for your child (no matter how good) if it conflicts with the team's mission.

You opt to have your child play competitive swimming in a particular organization. It pays to know what the game of competitive swimming (and your particular team) is all about, so that your child can get the most out of his, and your, investment, and so that you can best support the program and the team in order to enrich your child's experience.

PART III
COACH, PARENT, and SWIMMER

Collaborate for Success

You and your swimmer's coaches both want the same things for your swimmer that he wants. All of you want your swimmer to have fun, to swim fast, to win, to develop good habits, to acquire good life skills, to get and stay fit, and to benefit constantly from this lifestyle he continually chooses. Remember that.

You, your swimmer, and his coach, all play different roles in your child's swimming development, but all of you should be acting in concert to move in the same direction. Keep this in mind in your interactions with your swimmer and with his coach. Collaborative action will go a long way toward enhancing your child's swimming experience.

Chapter 5

The Coach's Role

To provide expertise

Ultimately your child is responsible for his swimming, but his coach is there for him. The coach is the most important resource available to your swimmer in his quest for swimming excellence.

Your swimmer's coach designs, manages, and supervises training; helps plan strategic race execution; teaches (or provides instructional resources for) technique, physiology, and psychology; and sets standards for performance and behavior. He is a swimmer's teacher, manager, sounding board, guidance counselor, partner, and head cheerleader.

The coach's role does not call for him to be your swimmer's friend or parent. Rather, he is an expert resource person. One who is closely involved in your child's development and your child's life, but your swimmer's coach is merely a resource nonetheless.

Your swimmer's coach cannot make your swimmer succeed. Your swimmer has to do it himself. All the coach can do is provide your swimmer with the opportunity to succeed.

The coach is a tremendous resource, truly the expert in this arena. Expect your child's coach to be available as an expert resource person and to share this expertise; but remember, it is up to your swimmer to access and avail himself of this precious resource.

The coach cannot swim for your child. The coach cannot train for your child. The coach cannot make your child succeed. Your child's coach is merely an expert resource person whose expertise is shared for a fee. Your child must do it himself with, of course, the coach's guidance, instruction, and encouragement.

To promote good values

It should be important to you that the coach espouses, lives, and promotes values that are consistent with those you want your child to embrace. Your swimmer's values will be effected by the values embraced by the coach. Make sure you both are on the same track.

To treat your child with respect and dignity

At times, the environment surrounding the game of competitive swimming can become quite intense. Even though, especially at those times, imperfect persons sometimes act imperfectly; you should continually expect the coach to treat your child with respect and dignity and expect for him to demand that everyone else does so as well. (Of course, both you and your child should treat the coach with respect and dignity at all times as well.)

To provide and maintain an environment that is conducive to the pursuit and enjoyment of swimming excellence

Your swimmer will be responsible for the quality of his experience. It can be no other way.

Your swimmer can have a great experience no matter what is going on around him. So too can he fail to take advantage of the most wonderful of opportunities. It is up to him.

The locus of responsibility notwithstanding, the quality of your child's swimming experience will be molded in part by the team environment. The coach will be substantially responsible for creating and maintaining the team climate. Look to the coach to provide and maintain an environment that is conducive to the pursuit and enjoyment of swimming excellence.

To do it his way

Every coach has something to offer. Sure, some are better than others and some would be better for your child than others. No coach is perfect. No program is perfect. No coach or program is perfectly suited to your child. One thing is certain: the way for your child to get the most out of the program he is in is to buy into that program.

Shop around. You want to buy the best. Once you settle on a program, however, remember that there are a lot of different ways to climb a tree. Please take note as well, that if someone jumps from one way to the treetop to another, he tends to move sideways, not upward; and he very well may fall out of the tree.

Trust your coach to find a way to the top. Then support his way.

Coaches plan. Programs have flow to them. They build upon the parts. In order to derive the most out of his swimming, your child should be encouraged to listen to his coach. You should encourage your swimmer to believe in the program—to buy it in its entirety; not to pick and choose pieces divorced from the whole.

To earn a good salary

Historically, coaches were volunteers. But in those days, amateur coaches spent a little time providing an activity for amateur athletes.

Times have changed. The demands on a coach have increased voluminously. Coaches work incredibly long hours, doing split shifts, working odd hours and weekends, with little time for family or social life.

They are expected to be totally dedicated, experienced, knowledgeable, polished professionals exhibiting considerable up-to-date technical expertise, infinite patience, tremendous stamina, and good humor. They are expected to act, not only as swimming professionals, but CEOs, labor, management, recruiters, and customer relations representatives all at the same time. They must not only perform consistently well day-in and day-out, but get scores of children to produce at least quality, if not superlative, competitive performance upon demand, under any conditions, against formidable opponents, while seeing to their charges' preparation, development conduct, and enjoyment at all times. If not sainthood, at least they deserve a good salary.

You merely may see a coach on deck, seemingly enjoying an exciting game with a great bunch of children. What you do not see is all the preparation and management time he puts in so that your children get the opportunity to play and to play well.

Don't begrudge coaches good salaries. They deserve to get paid well. Moreover, a good salary will provide incentive and attract, and keep, better coaches, ensuring a more quality experience for your swimmer.

Chapter 6

The Parent's Role

To provide and facilitate the opportunity

Your main role as a swimming parent is to provide your child with the opportunity to pursue swimming excellence. This means you actively play a supportive role.

You help most by providing your swimmer with transportational, financial, nutritional, and emotional support. It is up to you to facilitate all that it takes for your youngster to be in a position to squeeze every ounce of value out of this precious opportunity.

To provide financial support

As do most things of value, the opportunity for your child to swim costs money. Pools must be rented, insurance paid, experts hired, supervision assured, and equipment supplied. This all takes money.

Though many teams are non-profit organizations, they still require substantial capital to run. Most often parents are asked to pay the freight. Accept that one of your main roles will be to provide financial support.

To provide transportation

Whether it is driving him to practice, participating in a car pool, giving him bus money, or providing him with a car, gasoline, and insurance so he can drive himself; a large part of your role will be to provide transportation. Your swimmer cannot swim unless he can get to the pool.

With trips to and from the pool, on so many days (sometimes two or, occasionally, even three times per day), year round, this transportational commitment can be huge, expensive, and time consuming. It also can be fun and rewarding.

When my older son became of legal age to drive, he became one of the only teenagers in Texas who did not want to get his driver's license. One of his stated reasons was that he liked the time we spent together when I drove him to and from practice. He did not want to give up our time together. Only after I told him that I valued our time together as well and that after he got his driver's license, if he wanted, I would still drive him to practice, was he willing to get his license to drive.

To provide emotional support

One of your most important contributions to your child's swimming experience will be to provide emotional support. Be there for your swimmer.

Be there to listen whether he's thrilled, frustrated, disappointed, confused, confident, nervous, or lost. You don't necessarily have to say anything. Your child can find his way. You merely need to be there and to care.

Let your child know you enjoy the sport. Let him see how much you enjoy watching him swim, watching him compete, and watching him develop.

Enjoy his passion for the sport, his quest for excellence, his acceptance of the challenges, and his personal development.

Be your child's personal support staff, head cheerleader, and fan club. Be there for him.

To love your swimmer unconditionally

You love your child. Remember that.

Don't allow your expression of your love for him to fluctuate with his swimming performance. Express your love unconditionally. Show your swimmer that you love him no matter how well he swims.

Of course, as in any environment, this does not mean you should accept anything and everything your child does. Some behaviors are unacceptable and should not be tolerated without consequence. It just means that you should not withhold or withdraw, even temporarily, your love for your child as a consequence for substandard swimming performance.

To value the competitive swimming experience

What you value will be apparent in your support, or lack thereof. Decide to value the pursuit of swimming excellence and the skills, fitness, power, stamina, attitude, and challenges swimming will bring to your child. Demonstrate how much you value all the benefits derived from the pursuit of swimming excellence.

To make the decisions that allow consistency

Development takes time. It does not happen in one practice. Skills, power, stamina, and expertise all come with the cumulative effects of collective activity. Consistency is vital to success.

For your swimmer to best reap the riches swimming offers, you have to value the competitive swimming experience enough to support the decisions that allow consistency. Your swimmer will have to make it to practice with extraordinary consistency in order to best pursue excellence. Your support in making swimming a priority is vital.

Swimming success is not dependent upon sacrifice. There are no sacrifices made for swimming. Swimming success is dependent upon choice: choice in terms of directing action and of allocation of time, effort, and resources. Sometimes the choices are difficult, but the choices that lead to success are choices made based on predicted long-term benefit over those made based upon convenience, momentary whim, competing alternatives, or short term gratification. Some of these decisions will be parental ones. Your swimmer's success will be heavily dependent upon family decisions you make that afford him the opportunity to consistently pursue swimming excellence.

To allow your child to own his swimming

Whose swimming is it anyway? Do you want your child to get fit, learn skills, have fun, and gain all the other benefits competitive swimming has to offer; or are you trying to experience the thrill of competition and the accolades that come with success through him? Are you trying to recapture lost experiences, correct your mistakes, or vicariously make up for your lost opportunities?

It is your swimmer's swimming, not yours. Yes, be his support system. Provide him with this wonderful opportunity. Help him to take advantage of the swimming experience. Contribute with your support, excitement, wisdom, experience, and perspective; but let his swimming be his.

Let him own his mistakes, failures, and, most importantly, his successes. Let him rejoice in his accomplishments and feel disappointed with his failures. Let him own his swimming.

To create and maintain a positive environment at home

As your swimmer gets older, he should assume increasing responsibility for his swimming. Nevertheless, you still have a lot of wisdom, experience, and perspective to share. Your value system remains paramount. And, as long as your child is a dependent minor, you make the rules. Create and maintain an environment at home that will foster your swimmer's pursuit of excellence.

To promote good sleep habits

Swimmers train incredibly hard. They need rest. Moreover, if you are reading this, the odds are your swimmer is still growing. He needs sleep to grow.

The amount of sleep he gets is important. When he gets his sleep may be even more important. Eight hours sleep from 3 a.m. to 11 a.m. for a teenager accustomed to sleeping from 9 a.m. to 5 a.m. does not do the job. A consistent bedtime facilitates the benefits of sleep.

For younger swimmers that may mean that you set boundaries for bedtime. If you can avoid it, don't keep young athletes up late for your convenience.

Teenagers need to take more responsibility for their own well-being. They, however, still need limits. A curfew may help. Letting your teenager suggest a reasonable curfew to be negotiated is often the best way to set one. His suggested curfew may even be as early, or earlier, than you would have set.

To provide good nutrition and to promote good eating habits

Swimmers burn an enormous amount of calories. They need to eat a lot. But what they eat is tremendously important. They need high-octane fuel to perform. You do not want to feed low-grade fuel, full of contaminants, to a highly-tuned engine. Your swimming machine needs pure, rich fuel in order to perform at his peak and to keep from breaking down.

While swimmers need plenty of fuel, they do well not to carry excess weight. Excess weight will slow them down. They need good nutrition and lots of it, but they will not meet this need with foodstuffs filled with empty calories and high fat content. Make a wide variety of nutritious, healthful foods available, while limiting the availability of junk food.

To remind your swimmer to stay hydrated

Swimmers sweat when they train. Often, however, they don't realize it. Just as your highly sophisticated swimming machine needs pure, rich fuel, he needs to stay lubricated. Make sure your child drinks enough both at home and during swimming practice.

Provide him with a water bottle to take with him to practice. Encourage him to use it during training in order to stay hydrated. Make sure he knows to drink before he gets thirsty. And, keep him constantly hydrating at home.

To minimize stress

Optimal training for competitive swimming often entails walking a very fine line between stressing the body enough to stimulate maximum adaptation, but not so much that it breaks down. Other kinds of stress tend to deplete the body's resources and lower the body's immune system, thereby acting to diminish your swimmer's ability to take his training to a higher level and to avoid overtraining.

The physical stress that accompanies playing the game of competitive swimming is large (and for the most part quite healthy and enjoyable). Emotional stress, however, takes its toll. Help your swimmer to create and maintain a relatively stress-free home environment. Help your swimmer to keep school, relationships, and other areas of his life under control, enjoyable, and relatively stress-free.

To encourage your swimmer to keep up with his school work

Guide your swimmer to keep up or, better yet, to stay ahead in school. Otherwise there will be times when he will fall behind in his school, his swimming, or both; subsequently engendering stress.

Swimming is a great impetus for him to learn unusual success strategies that otherwise are not learned and are even socially frowned upon by the unmotivated masses. Use the impending benefit to your youngster's swimming to introduce him to weird ideas, such as: it is all right to read ahead; it is okay to turn a paper in before it is due; and it is permissible to ask the instructor what assignments loom ahead and to go ahead and get started on them.

To promote education in swimming

The more your athlete knows about his sport and about the ingredients and recipes for success, the more likely he will be to succeed, the greater will be his interest, and the more likely he will be to enjoy his swimming. Provide him with a rich array of educational materials.

Expose your child to the history of swimming, perhaps through The International Swimming Hall of Fame. Make available books, videos, subscriptions to swimming magazines, and other resources on the sport of swimming, its techniques, philosophies, psychology, and current events. All of these will enrich his opportunity to develop greater swimming expertise.

Of course, some resources are better than others. Some are superb, some relatively worthless. Some are neither good nor bad, but merely are good or poor fits with your swimmer's coach's program. Thus, it often is a good idea to check with your swimmer's coach for his recommendation on preferred resources.

To share your expertise, wisdom, values, perspective, and experience about life

Your swimmer's coach is the technical and strategical expert in this game. Your role is a supportive, not a directive one. You are wise to let the coach coach.

On the other hand, you have much experience, wisdom, and expertise about life. You are the keeper of your family's values, traditions, morals, and ethics. It is incumbent upon you to teach the values you embrace to your children and to protect these values from others' attacks.

To help to keep swimming in perspective

Sometimes it will seem as if swimming is not a metaphor for life, but rather that life is a metaphor for competitive swimming. The pursuit of swimming excellence requires much in the way of commitment, consistent goal-oriented action, and diligent attention to detail. It requires that a swimmer's goals and his action for excellence be highly valued with great consistency.

Competitive swimming is a wonderful, valuable, enriching, and rewarding lifestyle. The pursuit of excellence is a tremendously valuable passion. At the same time, swimming is just a game. You are the keeper of perspective.

Perspective promotes the freedom inherent in the sense of an "already-got-a-lot, nothing-to-lose, and lots-more-to-gain" approach that promotes consistent action for excellence and the risk-taking behavior that dares to do great things.

To teach your child to value his goals (including: "to win") differently from different temporal perspectives

There is no law that says one must value his goals equally from different points in time. It makes better sense to value one's goals tremendously highly while looking ahead and to give them little value retrospectively.

When your child is preparing for the game, and while he is playing, he should give his goals (including: "winning the game") enormous value. Preparing for the game and playing to win are what he is doing at those moments. He should attribute tremendous importance to what he is doing; it is the only thing he is doing right then.

As soon as the game is over (whether or not he won), the outcome does not have to be important anymore. In fact, it does not make much sense to hold on to valuing his goals. Regardless of whether or not he reached his goals, he can no longer do anything about reaching them. The game is over.

If he won or otherwise reached his goals, fine. Let him celebrate a little; then, urge him to set new goals and get back in the game. If he failed to win or otherwise reach his goals, too bad. It is okay for him to temporarily feel a little disappointment, but then urge him to set new goals and to get back in the game.

In any case, swimming is just a game. It is never life and death. It is never catastrophic. It is never all there is. Competitive swimming enriches one's life, it is not one's life. Help your child to determine competitive swimming's place in his life. Teach him to value his goals (including winning) differently from different temporal perspectives.

To help to keep swimming fun

When you send your swimmer off to practice, tell him to "have fun." When your swimmer gets home from practice, ask him if he "had fun." When you send your swimmer off to a meet or to race at a meet, tell him to "have fun." When your swimmer gets home from a meet or when you see him after a race, ask him if he "had fun." When you do, you are doing a great job as a swim parent.

To promote the enjoyment of the pursuit of swimming excellence

If you are going to do anything, you may as well make it fun. If your child is going to swim, he ought to make the pursuit of swimming excellence fun.

Don't let the pursuit of excellence get in the way of enjoyment. But don't promote, or accept, letting the fun get in the way of the pursuit of excellence. Your child will only lose out that way. Promote the value of making the pursuit of swimming excellence fun.

To remind your swimmer that it is his responsibility to make swimming fun

Okay, what do you do if you ask your swimmer, "Did you have fun?" and he says, "No!"? Then ask him, "Why not? Why didn't you make it fun? Why would you be willing for it to be anything but fun?"

When you put the onus on him for his failure to make it fun, you remind him of his ownership. You allow him to take responsibility for his own experience of his swimming. You suggest to him that the fun is in his hands and that he is fully capable of enjoying his swimming. You help him to build the skills that allow him to make whatever he is doing fun and to assume responsibility for his experience of his world.

Sometimes a swimmer will assess his enjoyment of a race based on the outcome. Actually, this is quite common—quite common, but also quite silly. One cannot legitimately determine his enjoyment of an act after the fact. One either enjoys an act or one does not—during the act. After it is over, one can enjoy the outcome or make it distasteful if he wants, but that does not alter one's original experience of the process.

Of course, a swimmer can affect his experience by periodically evaluating his performance while swimming. If your swimmer thinks he is doing well, he may be more likely to label what he is doing as fun, to get absorbed in the race, and to catch the flow; subsequently enjoying it more. If he is doing poorly, he may be less likely to label the experience as fun, and will be more likely to be distracted from the task at hand, thereby interfering both with enjoyment and performance, further exacerbating the problem. Either way, evaluative thinking is at least temporarily distracting. Swimmers are better off remaining task-oriented, concentrating on their goals, on their strategies, and on directing their performances.

Although there is much about swimming that is intrinsically fun, a swimmer's fears or his inattention to the value can mask the inherent fun. You aid both his enjoyment and his performance by redirecting him to the value of swimming, by telling him to "have fun." *

Your swimmer has a choice. He can make his swimming fun. He can make it drudgery. He can make it boring. He can make it thrilling. It is up to him.

---

* Allaying his fears is another issue.

Unfortunately, most children, especially these days, expect to be entertained. They are not accustomed to taking an active role in their own enjoyment. Nor are they generally aware of whose responsibility it is to make it fun. They do not know they have the option. They are not used to actively taking responsibility to make it happen.

You can help your swimmer to understand. Tell him to "make it fun." Ask him if he "had fun." If he claims he did not have fun, ask him why he did not make it fun. If he was bored or did not like it, ask him why he would choose to make it boring, unpleasant, or unrewarding. Let him know it is okay if he wants to get bored, but it seems like a poor choice to you: it is not fun, it does not feel good, and it is not productive to make swimming boring. Help him to understand that enjoyment is something he does, not something he receives.

To help your swimmer to value the challenges

Much of what is to be gained from the opportunity inherent in a competitive swimming environment comes from valuing the challenges. Much of the opportunity lost comes from avoiding the challenges, failing to enjoy them, or both.

Fitness comes from seeking out, tackling, and conquering (or even failing to conquer) the extremely tough physical challenges.

The competition, especially the worthy opponent, sets the standard for greater effort, better preparation, and a better game (even if it is just someone else with whom to play).

Help your swimmer to value the challenges. Challenges are good. The tougher they are, the better.

To criticize the act, not the person

Your child is human. As such, he is imperfect, fallible, prone to err. He will, at least occasionally, make mistakes, make poor choices, and fall short of his goals and your expectations; none of which, however, makes him a lesser person. These failures are merely his acts. They do not determine his worth, his value as a person, his Self.

It makes sense to judge performance. Such judgments are integral to learning, to providing incentive, and to directing future performance. Performance assessment provides direction for correction, improvement, and minimization—if not elimination, of mistakes. It provides information for restructuring goals, which, in turn, provides direction and incentive.

On the other hand, it does not make sense to judge your child. You cannot judge him accurately. Any judgment of him will be flawed. It will be an over-generalization, often based on a few performances, or even a single performance, under one particular set of circumstances, at a single moment in time.

Judgments of your swimmer not only will be wrong, but they will have no utility and may damage your child and your relationship with him. Judgments of personal worth will only cause problems.

Such judgments lead your child to expect that he will be judged based on his performance on other occasions. These expectations, in turn, engender performance anxiety, and its accompanying fear and nervousness. They will impair enjoyment, chip away at confidence, and evoke avoidance behaviors. They will elicit excuses, lies, attempts to put things in a more flattering perspective, blame, displays of anger, tears, other emotional upsets and outbursts, unwarranted remorse, and futile promises to do better that are merely designed to fend off your attacks. The threat of judgement elicits attempts to look good, or, even worse, to avoid looking bad, instead of the value for doing well that promotes action for excellence—all of which takes much of the fun out of the game.

Your child is not hot stuff when he does well. (Neither, by the way, are you when he does well.) Nor is he less worthwhile, let alone the worthless piece of you-know-what that you can lead him to feel as though he is when you criticize him for performing poorly. (Again, neither are you.)

Your child is not a good person. He is not a bad person. He is just a person—a person who performs well sometimes and poorly at other times. His worth cannot be measured; it certainly cannot be measured based on performance under some set of circumstances at a given moment in time or even on a series of such events.

I suspect that your child's worth to you is immeasurable, immeasurably large. Remember that. Show your value for him, this fallible human being that you love.

Don't criticize your child. Among other things, personal criticism suppresses risk taking behavior: behavior that is necessary, if he is to discover ways to succeed. Criticize the act, not the person.

To provide your swimmer with the freedom to improve

Persons are not static. They are ever-changing. While some behaviors are pretty well-ingrained, actions can be elicited, modified, prompted, directed, and guided.

Your child may respond to different situations fairly similarly, but both the responses and the situations can be changed. Moreover, new responses can be introduced.

Don't create expectations by overgeneralizing his actions, acting as if they are traits, qualities, or indelible habits. Allow your child the freedom to experiment. Give him the confidence to explore new approaches. Help him to find a way to make it happen.

Don't label your child. Don't put him in a nonchangeable box in which he may learn to dwell or from which he must struggle to get out in order to explore other possibilities. Give him the freedom to improve.

To provide pats on the back rather than kicks in the butt

Sometimes it seems as though your swimmer needs a good kick in the butt, or at least conventional wisdom would lead one to believe so. But conventional wisdom is often wrong, especially when applied to such unconventional things as the pursuit of excellence.

A kick in the butt carries so many dysfunctional messages: "I'm angry at you." "You're in trouble." and "You're bad." or, worst of all, "You're worthless." There is some value in a kick in the butt, but not in these messages which are carried within. The value of a kick in the butt lies in the other implicit messages ("Pay attention." "That wasn't good enough." "You can do better." and "I care.")—messages that tend to get lost, confused, and missed when presented in the company of threats and emotion.

There are other ways to show you have confidence and that you care without the emotion and the attack on your child's worth that comes with a kick in the butt. A strategically placed pat on the back works so much better to push swimmers forward.

A kick in the butt may seem to work temporarily. Nevertheless, while it may effect a forward lunge, it is more likely to cause a fall, ultimately yielding a major impediment to the desired progress and taking a huge bite out of the feast of swimming enjoyment.

Notice what your child does well. Let him know about the good actions you see him take. Keep patting him on the back. It will help to propel him forward.

To help your swimmer to act purposefully

Most swimmers go to swim practice because that is what they do at that time of day. They approach each practice with little purpose in mind. For that matter, most swimmers are not aware of, do not understand, and fail to take good advantage of the particular opportunity afforded to them. They do not know where they are, the nature of the opportunity presented, and how to best take advantage of the situation. They often either have not decided what they want or examined if what they want fits with where they are and what they are doing. And even if they have goals, they often are not attentive in the moment to their goals and to their purpose in swimming.

Help your child to understand, and to stay aware of, his mission and its benefits. Help him to act consistently with purpose.

Chapter 7

The Parent's Role in Helping to Create and Maintain a Positive Team Environment

To let the coach coach

When you signed your swimmer up, you hired a professional to coach your child. Let the coach coach. You do not hire an accountant to do your taxes, then do them yourself. You do not secure the services of a surgeon, then perform the surgery yourself.

Find a program for your child that has a professional coach. Then let the coach do his job. Most club swimming coaches are experienced and trained in the sport.

As is everyone, coaches are imperfect. But, unless you are a swimming coach yourself and are up-to-date on the latest techniques and theories, more than likely swimming coaches have greater expertise in this area than you do. Moreover, you have a very powerful something that coaches do not have: a conflict of interest. Your judgment is clouded in this arena by your love for your child. Your child's coach should care about your swimmer, but he will be more likely to be objective about your child's swimming than you are likely to be. Do your child a favor. Let the coach coach.

To allow the coach to coach without your constant scrutiny

Don't look over your coach's shoulder. What if the swimming coach showed up at your place of employment and watched everything you did all day? Would everything you do be perfect? Would the purpose and long-term benefit of everything you do be apparent to this lay person? Would you do things the way he would think they should be done or the way he would do them? Would his needs or particular project always take precedence over all of your other responsibilities? Would his scrutiny be distracting and obtrusive?

Yes, coaches are imperfect. No, coaches do not coach the way you would or the way you want them to. No, your child is not, and should not, be the center of the coach's universe. Moreover, everything looks different under the microscope and with constant scrutiny.

Let the coach coach without a critical audience. Don't look over his shoulder.

To allow the coach to coach without interruption

Don't interrupt the coach on deck. If you want to talk with the coach, do so during office hours. He cannot be managing practice, watching stroke technique, and instructing swimmers while you are talking with him.

To recognize that you have one, the coach has many

While you are focused on your child, the coach is responsible for the entire program. Though most coaches care about each and every swimmer, they must do what is best for the entire program. Most often that will also be what is best for your child, at least in the long run; but not always. Sometimes your child's immediate interests must come second to the long-term benefit of the overall program; but then, that too is most often in your child's long-term best interest.

Yes, all of us want our children to get to swim on the relay. Relays are fun. But only four swimmers get to swim on each relay. Often, the four swimmers who have demonstrated, in one way or the other, that they are likely (likely, not certain) to swim the fastest will get the nod, but not always. Sometimes, the coach (yes, it is his call) will use the opportunity to swim on a relay as a way to encourage good training habits, to reward practice performance, to give a child a special opportunity, to dole out shares of opportunity, to build confidence, to provide practice for performing in pressure situations, or for one of many other purposes. More than likely there is some purpose to the coach's decision on who swims on which relay. Respect it.

If you are concerned that your child is getting short-changed, talk to the coach at some future, mutually-convenient, scheduled time. Waiting for an appropriate time will be less disruptive, less likely to embarrass your child, and more likely to get you viewing the relay with perspective. There are always more relay legs to be filled in future meets.

To make a contribution to the team

Do what you can to support the team. Your participation in fund-raising, chaperoning, organizing social activities, assisting with travel arrangements, helping with equipment, running meets, and other support activities strengthens the program while letting your child know that you care and are there for him. Moreover, anything you can do to relieve the coach of administrative and support activities frees him up to spend more time on planning and technical areas.

At the very least, do not disrupt the program. Get your swimmer to each practice on time. Let the coach coach without interruption. Keep informed so that the coach does not have to repeatedly answer the same question. Get your entries in on time, so time is not spent chasing you down.

Consider that there are quite a few members on the team. If even a small percentage of them cause a disruption once in awhile, the cost (in terms of coaching or administrative time and in terms of diversion from the mission) is huge.

To promote the program

Your advocacy goes a long way. Say nothing but good things about your swimmer's team, the staff, team members, other parents, and, especially your children. Go out of your way to advocate the program, and all associated with it, to your child, to other parents, to the swimming community, and to the community at large.

Look for the good things and talk about them. Draw attention to the positive aspects of the program.

Yes, there will be imperfections. No program is perfect. But you are far better off (and so is the program and, as a result, your child) if you attend to, and comment on, the good.

To applaud good performance

Applaud good performance and effort (meaning action toward excellence). Cheer any good race or good swim whether by your swimmer, his teammates, or anyone else. Draw attention to the pursuit of swimming excellence.

To accept everyone associated with the team

It is unlikely that all of the swimmers on the team will like each other. It is more likely that some will not. There may even be one, two, or a few youngsters that no one likes. It does not matter. It matters very much, however, that they treat each other with respect and dignity, support each other, challenge each other, expect each other to make a contribution, and reinforce each other's action for excellence. Most importantly of all, it is imperative that every swimmer accept each and every other swimmer's right to participate in his team's pursuit of swimming excellence and his right to enjoy the quest. This is one of the basic foundations of a great program.

Similarly, you need to recognize that every swimmer, parent, coach, support staff person, and volunteer member has a right to participate in the program. You do not have to like everyone or anyone. You merely need to accept everyone associated with the team.

To expect others to support the team's mission

You should accept everyone's right to participate. But that does not mean you need to be accepting of everything everyone does.

Do not let anyone detract from the program. Help everyone involved to stay on track and to contribute to the team's pursuit of swimming excellence.

To be part of the solution, not the problem

Don't complain about the program or the coach. Complaints are cancerous. They eat away at all that is good and worthwhile.

Complaints draw attention to imperfections and get others focused on these failures instead of on what is working. For that matter, complaints often point to something that has nothing wrong with it and label it as bad, making it bad by the very act of complaining about it.

Your child's team will have imperfections. Often, there will be some aspect of the program that may not be perfectly suited to your liking. The coach will act differently than you may have if you were in his position or from how you may have wished he had. He will say things in a different way than you would and even than you would like him to. (Of course, even you often talk to your child, and otherwise act toward him, in ways other than you would like to act.) But don't complain about imperfections. Instead, make a contribution to the program.

If it is your perception that something is wrong, point it out only if something can be done about it and solely to someone who can do something about that which concerns you. If, and when, you do voice a concern, also offer a suggestion for corrective action. Contribute. Don't complain.

Chapter 8

Your Bargain With Your Swimmer

Is what you are willing to do contingent upon what he does?

Most swimming parents I talk with are willing to invest a lot of time and resources into providing this wonderful swimming opportunity to their children. If they were not, I probably would not find them among the pool of swimming parents in the first place. There are limits, however, as to what you are willing to invest. It pays to be explicit with yourself as to where you draw the line.

Is your level of investment contingent upon his? Are you willing to drive him to morning practice only if he sets his alarm, gets up, and wakes you up?

Is your continuing investment contingent upon his expression of appreciation for the opportunity? Does it vary with his performance or the diligence of his preparation?

Is your willingness to support him contingent upon his taking advantage of the opportunity? Does your swimmer earn the privilege to swim by doing his chores or otherwise helping out at home? Must he take care of other responsibilities? Must he do well at school? Must he act respectful of others?

What do you expect your child to do?

What expectations do you have for your child with respect to his swimming? Do you expect him to appreciate the opportunity you provide for him, to take advantage of this precious opportunity, to take responsibility for his swimming, to actively pursue excellence, to make it fun?

Do you expect your swimmer to contribute to the team? Do you expect him to embrace the the team's mission, to stay on track, to help others to keep on track, to actively protect the team environment, to treat others with respect and dignity?

Do you expect your swimmer to help you to be able to provide him with the opportunity? Do you expect your swimmer to appreciate your investments of time, money, and energy? Do you expect him to share his experience with you?

Do you expect that your swimmer will keep up with his other responsibilities? Do you expect him to do well at school, to help around the house? You should.

Competitive swimming is a great privilege and wonderful opportunity. Expecting him to continually earn the right to participate and to continually take advantage of this precious opportunity will help him to appreciate what he has and to take care of it. It will foster personal responsibility and help him to make his swimming his own.

Chapter 9

Your Swimmer's Role

To act responsibly

As cited earlier, you can lead a horse to water, but you can't make him swim a 200 fly. Your swimmer has ultimate responsibility for his swimming.

Help your child to understand that he is responsible for his swimming. He is responsible for his attendance, his performance, his equipment, his health, his fitness, his nutrition, and his enjoyment. Of course, you will want to take responsibility to help him to recognize his responsibility and to acquire the skills and knowledge he needs in order to assume his responsibility.

Younger swimmers will need more guidance and care. But no matter how old your swimmer is, he has an evolving role in his swimming that includes assuming increasingly greater responsibility as he moves toward independence.

Ultimately his swimming is his. He needs to value it, to take care of it, to act responsibly, and to own his swimming. When he fails, it is his responsibility. There is no one else to blame. Even if there were, it would do no good to assign blame to others.

When he succeeds, he needs to know that he did it. In fact, if he is to thrive, he has to do it himself. He must make it happen. No one else will, or can, do it for him.

Require your swimmer to act responsibly. He is responsible for his swimming, for his behavior, for his fate. No one else can do it for him.

To take care of other responsibilities

Swimming should not be cause for your swimmer to abdicate his other responsibilities. In fact, swimming excellence is supported by taking care of other responsibilities.

In the big meet situation, victory often goes to the one of the many well-trained, highly-skilled swimmers who best manages the environment in that high-pressure situation. By handling his role in the world around him and acting responsibly in all areas of his life, your swimmer will develop habits that will serve him tremendously well both in preparation for competition and at the moment of truth.

To take care of family responsibilities

Hopefully, you value the opportunity to pursue swimming excellence enough to structure your family life so as to furnish the support needed to provide your youngster with the opportunity not only to swim, but to commit himself to his swimming. When you do, you give him the best chance to grab from the treasure chest that adorns the pursuit of swimming excellence. Your support, however, should not be a license for your child to turn his back on family responsibilities. Quite the contrary. Learning to do what it takes to excel without neglecting family responsibilities contributes to swimming excellence.

Fortunately, most coaches highly value family. Most will tend to support your insistence that your swimmer meet his family responsibilities.

Your commitment to providing your child with the opportunity to swim, and the very fact that you are reading this now, both demonstrate your value for family. Pass this value on to your swimmer. Expect your swimmer to take care of his family responsibilities at all times.

To take care of his education

Totally immersed in the pursuit of swimming excellence is one of the best ways a youngster can spend his time. That does not mean, however, that swimming should supercede education. Swimming will provide an invaluable educational experience, but it is not a substitute for academic endeavors.

Fortunately, partly because of the environment swimming creates, partly because of the values its participants embrace, partly because of the skills (such as personal responsibility, goal setting, time management, and persistence) that swimming teaches, and partly because of the values typically espoused by their families, swimmers tend to do well in school. Your swimmer should too.

Many coaches take great pride in their swimmers' scholastic achievements. Many programs recognize their swimmers' academic success. Many coaches encourage swimmers to set goals for school as well as for swimming. And most coaches are acutely aware of the role that academic success plays in helping to place their swimmers into collegiate swimming programs. Many coaches, though one would think their jobs press in other directions, even value academic success over swimming performance.

Swimming should support your child's academic success. Expect your swimmer to take care of his education.

To value his swimming

The more your child learns (read: "chooses") to value his swimming, the better care he will take of it, the better he will swim, and the more he will enjoy his swimming.

Your swimmer should be expected, taught, and helped to value his swimming. Help him to choose to value it, to see it as good and as worthwhile. Help him to understand and to attend to the benefits and the fun derived from the pursuit of swimming excellence.

Then, teach, help, and remind him to act in a manner consistent with these values that you have helped him to embrace. Help him to keep his actions aligned with his value for competitive swimming, for the pursuit of excellence, for a lifetime of superlative fitness, for health, for goal-directedness, for competition, for the worthy opponent, and for all the precious aspects and ensuing benefits of the competitive swimming experience.

To consistently exhibit a positive attitude

It is easy to have a positive attitude. It is hard to have a positive attitude. It is easy to have a positive attitude because all a person has to do to exhibit a positive attitude is to value whatever it is he is doing; to act as if, to talk as if, and, hopefully, to think as if whatever he is doing is good and worthwhile. This is easily done.

It is hard to have a positive attitude because it is difficult to consistently attend to valuing what you are doing. Therein lies the challenge: to consistently exhibit a positive attitude.

To have a positive attitude toward his swimming, all your swimmer needs to do is to act, to talk, and, hopefully, to think consistent with a philosophy that says: "Swimming is good and more is better." and "Challenges are good and the tougher they are the better."

Expect your swimmer to consistently embrace a philosophy that says: "Swimming is good, the more the better.* Challenges are good, the tougher the better." When he consistently acts in a manner consistent with such philosophy, he has a positive attitude.

To take advantage of opportunity

Opportunity is always limited. It is there. Then it is gone.

Once an opportunity is lost, it can never be recaptured. There are no do-overs, no mulligans, and no second chances.

There may be additional similar opportunities. But once one has passed, it is gone. Moreover, each missed (or seized) opportunity affects future opportunities.

When your child misses a practice, for example, he not only fails to reap the gains from that practice, but, generally, he is not as prepared to take advantage of the next practice as he would have been had he made the one he missed. Then, because he is not as prepared for the next practice as he

---

* Of course, more swimming is not *always* good. There is a point of diminishing returns. Overtraining can be problematic. Your swimmer needs to take care to rest. Rest is a critical component of superlative preparation. Generally, however, "more is better" is a rule that works well to guide behavior that supports competitive excellence.

otherwise might have been, he cannot get as much out of the one after it, and so forth and so on.

Not only does your swimmer fail to gain from a missed practice, thereby bringing less to his next opportunity, but he also misses some of the flow of practice. Coaches plan for practices to build on one another, coordinate with one another, to tap into different energy systems on different days, and to build different segments of the ingredients for success at different times. Miss a practice and your swimmer misses the flow, some infrequently taught or practiced skills, or other aspects of the interrelated network of training opportunities.

Fortunately, no one ever takes advantage of all opportunities. No one ever prepares perfectly for a swimming race, and no one ever swims a perfect race. So, there is ample room for error. Your swimmer does not have to be perfect to excel, let alone to compete well. But he does gain tremendously from consistently taking better advantage of opportunity than do others.

Help your swimmer to value, to understand, and to take advantage of the opportunities that are presented to him and to those that he creates. He will not ever get another chance.

To make the commitment

A commitment is a big decision made in advance to make goal-oriented decisions. Without commitment, interest, behavior, and intensity fluctuate. There are always mediocre ways to approach swimming. There is always something else to do besides swimming.

Swimming is great fun and has much to offer. Reaping the rewards swimming offers, however, requires at least a modicum of consistency of good training. It requires consistently making the decision to take goal-oriented action. Such consistency is made likely by one big decision, made in advance, to decide to consistently take the goal-oriented option: the decision to commit to the pursuit of swimming excellence. Expect your swimmer to make the commitment to pursue swimming excellence.

To make progress

Expect your swimmer continually to take action to move forward. If your swimmer is standing still, he is likely to get passed by. And, he may very well get run over.

To stay on track

Swimmers generally are at practice because that is what they do at that time of day. Most lose sight of why they are there, where they are going, what they can do to reach their goals, what benefits await them, and whose responsibility it is to make practice productive and enjoyable.

Help your child to stay on track. Remind him what opportunity lies before him. Remind him of what a great opportunity he has each day. Help him to act in a manner consistent with his purpose. Remind him to make it fun.

To make the pursuit of excellence fun

Just as the program and its coaches should take care of making and keeping the pursuit of swimming excellence fun, so too should your swimmer. It is his responsibility.

Others may suggest that if something is not fun, one should not do it. I disagree. There are lots of good reasons to do things even if they are not fun. On the other hand, if one is going to do anything, he may as well make it fun.

Fortunately, with competitive swimming, it is easy to make it fun. There is much in competitive swimming that is inherently fun and little, if anything, about it that cannot be made enjoyable. Expect your swimmer to make the pursuit of swimming excellence fun.

Of course, as mentioned earlier, there is a huge difference between making the pursuit of excellence fun and having fun at the expense of the pursuit of competitive excellence. Your swimmer should be expected to make the pursuit of swimming excellence fun without letting the fun get in the way of his mission.

To choose to keep swimming interesting

Although most of competitive swimming is inherently fun, some will choose to make it boring or otherwise bad. For that matter, social mores will encourage and reward dissatisfaction and complaints.

Your swimmer has a choice. He can continually make his swimming fun and interesting or he can make any, or every, aspect of his swimming boring. It is up to him.

Boring is not fun. Boring is not productive. Boring does not feel good. To opt to make swimming (or most anything else—studies, for example) boring just is not a good choice. Unfortunately, most take a passive role. They do not know they have choices.

Remind your swimmer of whose responsibility it is to maintain interest and enthusiasm for his swimming. Expect him to keep his swimming interesting.

To make a contribution

Expect your swimmer to contribute to the program. Expect him to be a positive force helping to create an environment from which everyone (and most notably he) will benefit.

Expect him to accept, acknowledge, support, encourage, advocate, promote, challenge, and appreciate his teammates, coaches, staff, and volunteers. Expect him to compliment and applaud action for excellence. Expect him to be a good ambassador for the sport.

Expect your swimmer to know what he is there for and to stay on track, availing himself of this precious opportunity and consistently acting with that purpose in mind. Expect him to protect this invaluable opportunity, to help to keep others on track. Expect him to be a good role model, to act consistent with team policy, and to aid others in their quests.

Expect him to value the worthy opponent: Expect him to respect and appreciate the competition.

Expect your swimmer to contribute to making his team and this great sport even better.

To treat others with respect and dignity

You should expect your swimmer to treat everyone (including himself) with respect and dignity at all times. Not only is such behavior generally desirable, it is integrally important to making a contribution to creating and maintaining an environment that is conducive to swimming excellence. Moreover, if he treats others with respect and dignity, others are more likely to afford him the respect and dignity that he so richly deserves.

To swim to win

It has been said that it doesn't matter if you win or lose, it matters how you play the game. Personally, I think that it doesn't matter whether you win or lose, it matters that I win. Or, at least that is how I play the game. Your children should play that way too. Winning is the object of the game. It may not be who wins or loses, but how he plays the game that matters. The "how" to play, however, is to play to win.

Winning is not what the game is all about. There are greater reasons to participate. But winning is the object of the game. Your child will best reap the benefits of playing if he plays to win.

Winning is the object of the game. The pursuit of victory instills good values, produces useful habits, enhances skills, and promotes health and fitness. Pursuing victory is about preparing better and playing better than others. As such, the pursuit of victory promotes consistency, vigor, well-directed effort, strategy, and skill. Anyway, playing to win is more fun.

If your child prepares better, more consistently, with greater vigor, more well-directed effort, better strategy, greater skill, and greater enjoyment; he is more likely to win. If he plays to win: he is more likely to develop good habits, skills, and strategies; to produce greater fitness and health; and to have more fun. That, after all, is what really matters.

Isn't this the way the game should be taught—to play to win? Think about teaching a child to play chess. If a child is shown how to move each chess piece and then left to play, what does he get from playing? Well, most children would get bored quickly. Many would have enough sense to decide to organize the game by creating some object and setting some goal. To reach that goal would be said to win.

Of course, just giving a child a board, some chess pieces, and leaving him to play would not be providing him with a game. A game must have some object, some goal. To achieve that object or goal is to win. Different games have differing ways to play, different ways to win. But in all games, the way to play is structured to lead to victory, to achieve some goal—at least that is the object of the game.

Your child will get more out of playing if he acknowledges the true nature of the game, plays the game and plays it right, instead of trying to make it into something it is not. In other words, he will get more out of playing swimming if he will immerse himself in the vigorous, relentless, single-minded pursuit of victory—if he will play to win. (Of course, it is imperative that he manages to enjoy the pursuit of victory.)

There is tremendous value in playing to win. In fact, it is crucial that one plays to win in order to best reap the benefits of playing. That does not mean, however, that one must win in order to reap the benefits of playing. It matters how one plays. It matters that one plays to win. It does not matter anywhere near as much whether one wins.

Winning is the goal of the game, the goal that provides a game to play. Winning isn't everything. It is merely an excuse for the game; without this goal, there is no game to play. But even if it is not the reason to play, winning is the goal of the game. To play to win is the way to play. If your child is going to play, he will get the most out of the game if he plays to win.

PART IV
WHAT TO EXPECT

Chapter 10

The Natural Flow

Natural progress

At first, your young swimmer will improve quickly, in large increments, and almost every time out. With the acquisition of rudimentary skills, a modicum of conditioning, and the development of a little power; or just by growing; your child will show vast improvement in his swimming. In relatively no time at all, he will swim better and faster than can the vast majority of the world's population.

As his skill increases, technical refinements will be smaller. At some point, increased power will yield limited gains, maybe even reaching a point of diminishing returns. Eventually, your swimmer will stop growing.

As speed increases, improvement tends to be harder-earned and it tends to come less often and in smaller increments. It is the physics of the thing. The faster one goes, the greater the resistance of the water. And, with increased speed, the resistance of the water increases in a geometric rather than a linear manner. The faster one swims, the increasingly greater power it takes to propel the body through the water.

Furthermore, as your child gets faster, he tends to compete against increasingly tougher competition. That is the way the game is set up.

You can expect that your child will make tremendous progress rapidly. His success, however, may vary. It is an extremely rare swimmer who excels at an early age and continues to outdo the competition at all levels. It is more likely that your child's relative performance will vary.

Of course, one of the nice things about the natural progression of performance is that, although swimming, like every other activity, proves that life isn't fair, it tends to reward good preparation, persistence, and consistency. If your swimmer consistently prepares well over time, eventually he will tend to have at least a fair amount of success. And, of course, he will benefit greatly from the quest.

Children learn, develop, and progress at different, ever-varying rates

Everyone's body changes. Everyone goes through growing spurts. As each one does, the changes in each will be different. No two individuals are alike.

When your swimmer shoots up, his swimming may get a tremendous boost. With growth may come speed and power.

On the other hand, as he grows, he may struggle as he adjusts to the changes in his body. The growth spurt may exhaust him. He may have to grow into his body. He may not yet be strong enough to propel this newly enlarged vessel. It may take awhile for him to benefit from his growth.

His body may betray him. What was once a body ideally suited for swimming, may now be shaped poorly for this sport.

Swimmers' interests change. Their motivations vary.

Swimmers get tired. Pursuing swimming excellence requires walking the fine line between pushing the limits and overtraining. Sometimes your swimmer will cross the line. Then, his speed, motivation, interest, and/or moods will show that something is wrong. He is tired.

Sometimes the learning curve is steep. Sometimes it is flat.

In this competitive sport, your child will constantly be compared to others in a continually changing competitive environment. The more your swimmer improves, the tougher the competition he will have the opportunity to face.

Other swimmers will plateau, shoot ahead, quit, or star, generally covering the gamut of levels of performance and interest. It will neither seem fair nor understandable. It is just the way it is.

The game will change. His place in the game will vary. But no matter what, if your swimmer sticks with it, commits himself to the pursuit of excellence, and consistently makes the pursuit of swimming excellence fun, he will have the opportunity to reap huge benefits from this wonderful lifestyle.

Chapter 11

The Psychological Challenges

Fear of pain

As I pointed out earlier in this book, at the highest levels, swimmers train harder than do any other athletes in the world, repeatedly taking their bodies to places where ordinary human beings never go. Swimmers reap tremendous gains from their hard training, but they feel it. The internal events swimmers routinely experience are unimaginable to the uninitiated.

Swimmers are asked to challenge their bodies enormously, fairly consistently, for hours-upon-hours, day-in and day-out. When they accept the challenge, they opt for intense discomfort. Sometimes they experience the feel as exhilarating and they enjoy it. Often they battle with the discomfort. Frequently, they struggle with the decision to get after it, finding it hard to train at the level they want to train, because they are afraid it will hurt.

Handling the discomfort is one of the most formidable psychological challenges facing swimmers. The fear of pain interferes with the pursuit of swimming excellence. It makes it hard to make good decisions. The fear distracts the swimmer. And it makes it more difficult for a swimmer to enjoy what he is doing.

Fortunately, there is no pain in swimming. There are some intense sensations. There is much discomfort. But there is no pain.

Swimming, even when effort is intense, does not hurt. It does no biological damage. Quite the contrary, it fosters biological growth.

Most swimmers, and even most coaches, do not understand that the sensations experienced are deceiving, that although the sensations may be uncomfortable, they do not hurt. This is not an easy concept to get. As a result, fear of pain is one of the most formidable psychological challenges facing your swimmer.

Fear of failure

Failure is not worthy of your swimmer's attention. To give thought to failure is to distract from the task that looms ahead. But failure is a reoccurring part of the game. Your swimmer is going to fail—over and over again. It is the nature of the game.

The challenge looming before your swimmer is to overcome any fear of failure: to focus on striving for his goals rather than on the failures he wishes to avoid, and to learn from failure without letting it get in the way.

Don't make a big deal of failure. Swimming is just a game.

Failure, at least before the fact, is not worthy of attention. Your swimmer is better off concentrating on doing what it takes to reach his goals.

After the fact, there is not much use in worrying about having failed. Failure is merely the gap between expectations and experience. It is simply the difference between one's goals and one's performance. Furthermore, one certainly cannot change the outcome after the fact. The results stand. There is nothing one can do to change them.

Goals are substantially arbitrary. A goal is only an excuse for the game. It merely creates the game. If your child sets a goal, he gets to play. Though, if he fails, your child does not receive the spoils that go to the victor, he still can reap the enormous benefits that come with playing to win.

Failure is never the goal. It is not okay to fail. On the other hand, to have failed is okay. Certainly your child is okay when he has failed, even though he has failed.

When your child has failed, he has merely failed to reach some expectation. He has not demonstrated some inadequacy. The fact is that your child is not a failure, if he has failed. He merely failed—at that one particular moment in time—under those circumstances—with that level of preparedness—with the exhibited strategy. Surely if he had done anything differently, or if the performance had taken place at any other particular moment in time, the results would have been different.

Unfortunately, in our society we learn to judge each other (and subsequently ourselves) based on performance, usually weighing the most recently performed act most heavily. As a result, one's sense of worth, his very right to exist, tends to be determined by the quality of his performance.

We tend to judge ourselves more harshly in certain situations. For example, we tend to judge ourselves more harshly in situations where we care about our performance, where we have more invested in how well we do. If we do not care, well, we just do not care how well we do.

We tend to judge ourselves more harshly in situations where our performance is public. If we mess up in the privacy of our own rooms, it is no big deal. On the other hand, if we fail in front of thousands of spectators, the feeling is different.

We tend to judge ourselves more harshly when there is no luck involved. If there is luck involved, we can always say we were unlucky.

We tend to judge ourselves more harshly in situations where the performance is ours and ours alone. If it is a joint effort, we can always blame the other guy.

We tend to judge ourselves more harshly in situations where our performances are clearly measured. If no one can tell how well we do, we are safe. We can always say we did well.

We tend to judge ourselves more harshly in situations where the performance is measured objectively. If the results are determined by someone else's judgment, we can always say he was wrong. Well, look at competitive swimming. It is the epitome of the situation in which we judge ourselves the most harshly.

Swimmers tend to care very much about what they do. You and your swimmer both have a lot of time, effort, and money invested. Swimming is performed in front of a crowd. Coaches, teammates, friends, family, and lots of strangers are there to view the performance. At the biggest meets, there literally may be thousands of spectators present and millions more watching on television and through the Internet.

And talk about being exposed to the public, swimmers not only perform in front of large crowds, but they do so practically naked. They perform in suits that leave little to the imagination. The older swimmers even shave the hair off of their bodies for the big meets. They are not even buffered by body hair from exposure to the environment.

Here they are, practically naked, in front of all those folks, many of whom they know, doing this thing that they care very much about, with no luck involved, no judgment calls, swimming by themselves, with no one else on which to blame poor performance. And, the results of their performances are measured electronically to the hundredth of a second and posted on a big scoreboard in bright lights for all to see. If they are poised to judge their Selves based on their performances, it is no wonder that they get afraid.

They get confused. Instead of racing for the joy of the game, vying for a medal, a ribbon, a trophy, a title, or the like, they put their Selves on the line: their worth, their very right to exist. As a result, they can get afraid to fail.

Fear of failure can engender anxiety. Performance anxiety can interfere with the fun, block commitment, and can lead to excuses and avoidance. All the while, society keeps pushing the idea that one is only worth as much as his last performance.

But your child's performance is not a measure of his worth. It is merely a measure of how well he performed at that moment in time, under that particular set of circumstances, with some level of preparedness, utilizing some particular strategies. And even then, it is a crap shoot randomly rolled by the natural variance attributable to being human.

Swimming is something your child does (albeit a rich, rewarding something). It does not define his being. Certainly, your child's worth is not defined by his swimming performance.

The challenge before your swimmer is to learn to divorce his performance from his worth: to learn to judge what he does without judging his Self, even while continually being bombarded by the contrary expectations of society. It is a continuing challenge. And it is quite a formidable one.

71

Inattention

Swimmers want to swim fast. They want to win. They want to enjoy their swimming.

Unfortunately, they are not always attentive to their intentions. They get distracted or just forget what they are doing and why they are doing it.

From time to time they lose sight of their goals. They do not understand the importance of each opportunity because it is so hard to see the collective nature of their preparations.

Often they fail to pay attention to each of their responsibilities to find a way, to make it happen, and to enjoy every second of the process. They carelessly rely too much on their coaches. Or they act as though it will just happen with the passage of time, failing to see their own roles in producing success.

Sometimes they get led astray and dragged down by others who are inattentive, who do not value the opportunity, or who want to hold everyone back so that they will not look bad in comparison. Your swimmer constantly will have to deal with peer pressure.

Help your swimmer to stay on track. Help him to understand the purpose of practice, to know his coach has a plan, and to set goals for each week, each day, and each training swim.

Peer pressure

Very few persons value excellence. Most of your child's peers will not. They will, however, attempt to exert influence on your child's values and his behavior. Peer pressure will be a constant foe.

Peer pressure is a strong invitation from one's peers to act as they do: to act normal, average, mediocre. Left on its own, peer pressure almost inevitably pushes toward mediocrity. It virtually never promotes excellence.

One cannot act normal or average and win. In order to excel, your child needs to develop resistance to peer pressure and to hold value for acting different. Your swimmer needs to dare to act different, to stand alone and take goal-oriented actions in the face of influences that press for him to wallow in mediocrity. He will constantly face the challenge of others' attempts to dissuade him and distract him from his pursuit of swimming excellence.

Plateaus

When your child first starts swimming, progress comes quickly, easily, and in big chunks. A mere modicum of skill, power, and conditioning, coupled with growth and development, spurs increased speed. With experience, he learns pace and strategy. The bigger he gets, the more skill he acquires, the more power and stamina he develops; the faster he tends to swim. But the faster he swims, the harder it gets to swim even faster, the less often he tends to improve, and the more often improvement tends to come in harder-earned, smaller increments, if at all.

Sooner or later, your child's progress will seem to plateau. When it does, both you and he need to understand that at the higher levels of performance smaller improvements are more meaningful.

That is not to say that he cannot make big drops no matter how fast he has swum. He can. And, he should train to do so. But small, more slowly-attained improvements should not be cause for discouragement. They are merely part of the game.

Notice too, a plateau is a sign that your swimmer is progressing in small, unnoticed increments or that he is in a rut. It is not a sign that he has reached his peak and cannot improve any further.

PART V
THE MYTHS

Chapter 12

Don't Pave the Road With Good Intentions

"Be all you can be"

When you exhort your child to "be all you can be," it sounds good, but what exactly do you mean? Are you encouraging him to actualize his potential? You must imply something like that. That is a good intention, but again, what exactly do you mean?

How is potential measured? For that matter, can potential ever truly be measured?

Don't such challenges only imply limits? When you encourage your child to "be all you can be," you imply that there is some level he "can be" beyond which he cannot go. This cannot be useful. You do not want to limit your child's performance or have him start his quest with some implied limit in mind.

No one knows if there are any limits to how well your child might perform. Even if there are, we certainly do not know what they are.

Humans are ever-changing. Capacities change and fluctuate constantly, both internally and environmentally. That is a large part of what training is all about: creating skills, strategies, and physical adaptations that enhance performance. Success is a lot about finding a way: shaping a body and creating ways to propel it through the water faster than others.

No one knows where any possible limits to your child's performances might lie, but you can be sure that his capacities are constantly changing and can be increased. You also can be sure that any limits he may think he has will only limit his motivation, his preparation, his confidence, and, subsequently, his performance.

Don't encourage him to "Be all you can be." Encourage him to "Give it a go."

"Do the best you can"

Why in the world would you ever want your child to do the best that he can? Isn't there always room for improvement? What if he does the best that he can and it is not good enough?

When you tell your child to do the best that he can, you prepare him to fail. Isn't that what you mean: "Oh well, you probably won't win, but that's okay as long as you do your best."?

Aren't you essentially telling him to go out there, mean well, put forth effort, utilize his present skills and level of preparation, and fail? In essence, you imply that his best will suffice, even though it is not likely to be good enough to win. Or, at least, that his best is good enough, independent of how well he does.

One thing of which you can be sure, when you suggest to your child that he do the best that he can, you are suggesting that there is some limit to his performance (the best he can do) beyond which he cannot reach. Why not allow him to be unlimited in his aspirations?

Not everyone is going to win. Not everyone is going to do well in comparison to everyone else. But there is no evidence to suggest that anyone and everyone cannot improve upon past performances and present capacities, nor is it useful to think that one has reached his peak or even that he has some peak to reach. Why not encourage your swimmer to find a way to reach new speeds?

And who is to say that your child cannot win? Maybe if the door to victory is kept open, even a tiny crack, he will find a way to push through it.

"It's okay as long as you tried"

Have you ever told your swimmer, "It's okay as long as you tried."? If you are like most parents, you have. But when do you do so?

Let me put it another way. Have you ever said, "It's okay as long as you tried." to your swimmer after he performed brilliantly?

Of course you have not. If you have told your youngster "It's okay as long as you tried." at all, you have said it to him after he failed.

What does he learn when you tell him: "It's okay as long as you tried."? Well, basically he learns that it is okay that he failed, as long as he "tried." He learns that it is okay to fail, as long as he meant well or put forth effort or both.

Oh, the intentions are okay. You certainly mean well. You do not want your child to feel bad about himself or his performance. So, you console him with: "It's okay as long as you tried."

Yes, somewhere in there is the message that effort will eventually be rewarded. But is that really the case?

Well-directed effort increases the chances of success. But it increases the odds, it does not guarantee anything. The world is not fair. Not even the swimming world.

Of course the critical part of the phrase: "well-directed effort" is "well-directed." Effort alone does not get a swimmer where he wants to go. He maximizes his chances by exerting an optimal amount of effort in the right direction.

Moreover, too much effort can be counterproductive. Effort is an increase in muscular tension. Some effort helps. More effort often helps even more. However, all-out effort usually hinders performance.*

---

* There is a difference between "all-out effort" (meaning: "maximum exertion") and going all-out (meaning: "commitment"). Commitment usually serves to maximize performance. Maximum exertion does not.

There is such a thing as trying too hard. Maximum speed comes with optimal effort, not maximum effort. Maximum effort elicits diminishing returns. There comes a point beyond which more "try" (read: "increased effort") impedes performance.

"It's okay as long as you tried." means that it is okay that you failed (or really, that you are okay, even though you failed) as long as you put forth effort. But is it really okay to fail? And shouldn't it be a given that your child is okay even when he has failed. You do not ever want to put his worth at issue.

The reality is: it is not okay for him to fail "as long as he tries." (Though he certainly is okay even if he has failed, irrespective of whether he "tried.") You want your swimmer to succeed. You want him learn to do what it takes. You do not want him to learn to just try—to put forth effort and fail.

"What's wrong with you? You didn't even try"

"What's wrong with you? You didn't even try." has to be one of the worse things I ever hear parents say to their children.

When I hear this nonsense, I am frequently tempted to prompt swimmers to respond to this verbal attack by saying, "You're right. I didn't try. I thought I'd stink up the pool; embarrass myself, my family, my coach, and my teammates; impugn the integrity of the program; and make a mockery of the competition." But then, professionalism prevails and I refrain from teaching them to use sarcasm.

I have worked with more than 15,000 swimmers. All of them have told me that they want to swim fast and they want to win when they race. If, in fact, they do not "try," it is because they are scared, they feel hopeless, or they are inattentive to what they are doing. It is not because they do not want to do well.

Anyway, you do not really want your swimmer to try. You want him to succeed. To "try" is to fail. To "try" is to put forth some effort, but still fail. As was said in *Star Wars*: "Try not. Do or do not. There is no try."

Well-directed action, not effort, is what yields success. You do not help promote well-directed effort by telling your swimmer that there is something wrong with him. (Please note: "What's wrong with you?" is a rhetorical question, a statement disguised as a question that, in this case, says: "There is something wrong with you. You are bad.")

You want your swimmer to do well because you want good things for him. You want him to give it a good go, to muster all of his resources and parade out his best performance. But remember he cares too. He wants to do well.

He wants to swim fast. And he wants to win. Don't question his intentions. Don't put his worth at issue. Encourage him to get past the obstacles to success and to find a way to make it happen.

Or, better yet, play the ideal swimming parent. Just send your swimmer off with a "have fun."

Ten Rules
by which to
Parent Your Swimmer

1. Provide your swimmer with the best opportunity available.

2. Support your swimmer.

3. Create and maintain a positive environment at home.

4. Love and accept your child unconditionally. Criticize the act, not your swimmer.

5. Let your child own his swimming. It is his swimming, not yours.

6. Make a contribution. Support the team.

7. Make swimming a collaborative pursuit between swimmer, coach, and parent.

8. Let the coach coach.

9. Demonstrate your value for competitive swimming excellence. Encourage your swimmer to play to win, but remember it is just a game whereby most of the value stems from playing to win, not from having won.

10. Tell your swimmer to "have fun."

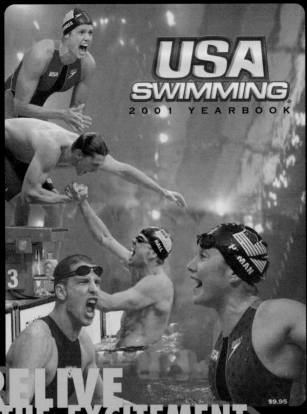

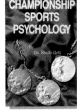
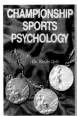

Did you borrow this book? If so, why not order one for yourself?

ORDER FORM

Please send the following books by **Dr. Keith Bell**:

___ copies of **The PARENT'S GUIDE** .... @ $11.95 _____

___ copies of **The SWIM TO WIN PLAYBOOK** .... @ $29.95 _____

___ copies of **The Nuts & Bolts of PSYCHOLOGY FOR SWIMMERS**.................. @ $11.95 _____

___ copies of **WINNING ISN'T NORMAL** .... @ $11.95 _____

___ copies of **WHAT IT TAKES: THE ABC'S OF EXCELLING** (hardcover) .... @ $19.95 _____

___ copies of **COACHING EXCELLENCE** .... @ $19.95 _____

___ copies of **YOU ONLY FEEL WET WHEN YOU'RE OUT OF THE WATER:**
Thoughts on Psychology and Competitive Swimming ..... @ $16.95 _____

___ copies of **CHAMPIONSHIP SPORTS PSYCHOLOGY** .... @ $21.95 _____

___ copies of **RELAXATION TRAINING (Cassette)** .... @ $11.95 _____

___ copies of **RELAXATION TRAINING (CD)** .... @ $14.95 _____

Subtotal Books: _____

(Please add 6.25% sales tax for every book shipped to a Texas address) **Sales Tax:** _____

SHIPPING & HANDLING
For single copy orders or first book please include $5.00 $5.00
___ additional copies of **The SWIM TO WIN PLAYBOOK** please add $4.00 per copy _____
___ additional copies of all other titles please add $1.00 per copy _____
___ number of copies being shipped outside the USA * please <u>add</u> $8.00 per copy _____
* Please remit International Money Order or check drawn off of a U.S. bank in U.S. dollars

Subtotal SHIPPING & HANDLING _____

TOTAL ENCLOSED: _____

NAME _____

ADDRESS _____

CITY _____ **STATE** _____ **ZIP** _____

PHONE _____ **EMAIL** _____

TEAM or ORGANIZATION _____

Make checks payable and send to: **KEEL PUBLICATIONS**
P.O. Box 160155
Austin, Texas 78716

512-327-1280 / books@swimdoc.com

PG

Contact us for wholesale & quantity prices.
Prices subject to change. See www.swimdoc.com for current price information.
Please allow approximately 2 weeks for delivery.

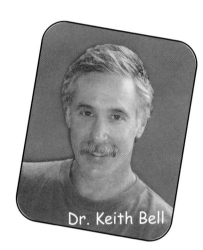